9/12

SandCastle™
Animal Groups

A Flock of Sheep

ANIMAL GROUPS
ON THE FARM

Alex Kuskowski

CONSULTING EDITOR, DIANE CRAIG, M.A./READING SPECIALIST

A Division of ABDO

ABDO
Publishing Company

visit us at www.abdopublishing.com

Published by ABDO Publishing Company, a division of ABDO, P.O. Box 398166, Minneapolis, Minnesota 55439. Copyright © 2013 by Abdo Consulting Group, Inc. International copyrights reserved in all countries. No part of this book may be reproduced in any form without written permission from the publisher. SandCastle™ is a trademark and logo of ABDO Publishing Company.

Printed in the United States of America, North Mankato, Minnesota
062012
092012

 PRINTED ON RECYCLED PAPER

Editor: Liz Salzmann
Content Developer: Nancy Tuminelly
Cover and Interior Design and Production: Anders Hanson, Mighty Media, Inc.
Photo Credits: Shutterstock

Library of Congress Cataloging-in-Publication Data
Kuskowski, Alex.
  A flock of sheep : animal groups on the farm / Alex Kuskowski.
    p. cm. -- (Animal groups)
  ISBN 978-1-61783-538-4
  1. Domestic animals--Behavior--Juvenile literature. 2. Social behavior in animals--Juvenile literature. I. Title.
SF75.5.K87 2013
  636--dc23
                        2012009029

SANDCASTLE™ LEVEL: FLUENT

SandCastle™ books are created by a team of professional educators, reading specialists, and content developers around five essential components—phonemic awareness, phonics, vocabulary, text comprehension, and fluency—to assist young readers as they develop reading skills and strategies and increase their general knowledge. All books are written, reviewed, and leveled for guided reading, early reading intervention, and Accelerated Reader® programs for use in shared, guided, and independent reading and writing activities to support a balanced approach to literacy instruction. The SandCastle™ series has four levels that correspond to early literacy development. The levels are provided to help teachers and parents select appropriate books for young readers.

Emerging Readers	Beginning Readers	Transitional Readers	Fluent Readers
(no flags)	*(1 flag)*	*(2 flags)*	*(3 flags)*

Contents

Animals on the Farm

Humans raise animals on farms. The animals are called livestock. Livestock is raised for food and money.

Many animals on farms live in groups. Farmers raise them all together.

Why Live in a Group?

Animals often live in groups. Animals in a group can **protect** each other. They can share space, food, and water. They also work together to help raise babies. Many animal groups have fun names!

A Flock of Sheep

On a farm, a group of sheep is called a flock. If sheep are frightened, they run away at first. Then they turn and face the danger as a group.

Sheep Names

MALE	FEMALE	BABY	GROUP
buck, ram	*ewe, dam*	*lamb*	*flock*

A Band of Horses

A group of horses is called a band. Horses are social. On a farm, they eat and drink together. For fun, they play and **gallop**.

Horse Names

MALE
stallion, stud

FEMALE
mare, dam

BABY
foal

GROUP
band, harras, herd

A Brood of Chickens

Chickens live together in a brood. They have a pecking order. Chickens higher in the pecking order are more important. They peck at lower chickens.

Chicken Names

MALE
rooster

FEMALE
hen

BABY
chick

GROUP
brood, flock

14

A Chattering of Chicks

A chattering of chicks is a group of baby chickens. After they **hatch**, chicks **huddle** together for **warmth** and safety.

Chick Names

MALE
cockerel

FEMALE
pullet

BABY
chick

GROUP
chattering, clutch, peep

A Herd of Cattle

A herd of cattle does everything together. When they are out in a field, they all eat at the same time. When they sleep, they all sleep at the same time.

Cattle Names

MALE	FEMALE	BABY	GROUP
bull	*cow*	*calf*	*herd, drift*

A Farrow of Piglets

A group of piglets is called a farrow. Piglets love to play. They have fun chasing each other.

Piglet Names

MALE
male

BABY
piglet

FEMALE
female

GROUP
farrow, litter

A Rafter of Turkeys

A group of turkeys is called a rafter. Turkeys watch out for each other with their **amazing** eyes. In daylight, turkeys have better eyesight than humans!

Turkey Names

MALE	FEMALE	BABY	GROUP
tom	*hen*	*poult*	*rafter*

More

FARM GROUPS

A clowder
of cats

A pack
of dogs

A drove
of donkeys

A mischief
of mice

A drift
of pigs

A herd
of alpaca

A trip
of goats

A swarm
of bees

Quiz

1. Horses are not social. *True or false?*

2. Chickens live alone. *True or false?*

3. Chicks **huddle** together for **warmth**. *True or false?*

4. Piglets have fun chasing each other. *True or false?*

5. Turkeys have bad eyesight. *True or false?*

Glossary

amazing – wonderful or surprising.

gallop – to run at the fastest speed possible.

hatch – to break out of an egg.

huddle – to crowd, push, or pile together.

protect – to guard someone or something from harm or danger.

warmth – the quality or state of being warm; heat.